Chocolate Cake and Other Losses

Chocolate Cake
and Other Losses

Poems about Grief

Shirley Biggerstaff Wright

FOREWORD BY
D. Kenneth Wright

RESOURCE *Publications* · Eugene, Oregon

CHOCOLATE CAKE AND OTHER LOSSES
Poems about Grief

Resource Publications
An Imprint of Wipf and Stock Publishers
199 W. 8th Ave., Suite 3
Eugene, OR 97401

www.wipfandstock.com

PAPERBACK ISBN: 978-1-6667-3607-6
HARDCOVER ISBN: 978-1-6667-9390-1
EBOOK ISBN: 978-1-6667-9391-8

11/07/22

Dedicated to

the love of my life: Ken

my children: Jonathan, Devi, Melanie

their spouses: Fairlight, Jessica, Mark

my grandchildren: Cora, Florence, Elizabeth, Grace, Matthew, Calvin, Maggie, Atticus, Oscar, Tallulah, Lily Mae, and Miles

Contents

Foreword

These poems reach out to take the reader by the hand offering moments for wholeness and hope. I have observed Shirley on many occasions holding the hands of parishioners in times of overwhelming grief, providing compassionate presence and prayers of assurance. I believe that that there was a strong sense of the presence of God with them. My confidence comes from personal experience. For over fifty years she and I have walked together hand-in-hand, with God, in abundant joy and in profound grief; we have persevered. Reading this poetry provides a blessed time of hope-filled peace.

—The Reverend D. Kenneth Wright, PhD.

Introduction

"Two things," they say, "are certain—death and taxes!" One of those realities is fairly easy to escape except as the 15th of April approaches each year. The other—our ultimate demises, our own deaths—stares us in our faces and requires the best of coping mechanisms. We practice it faithfully—denial.

For most of us most of the time, denial about our own deaths proves quite easy. Certainly when we are young, we feel rather invincible, but at some point in time, there are changes in health status that rattle our usual coping mechanisms. For me, that was a metastatic breast cancer diagnosis. My head began to spin with questions like, "What do I need to do to prepare? How can I help my family as the ultimate approaches? How do I spend my time in the meantime?"

It is a challenging grief experience—that of trying to prepare for one's ultimate end. I slipped into depression and wound up in my doctor's office in a puddle of tears. She encouraged me to begin journaling which ultimately led to my writing poems instead—the beginning of this volume.

Over time, especially as some of the initial trauma over my diagnosis subsided, I had time to reflect on many other grief experiences of my life but also upon the many different grief experiences of parishioners over the course of my work as a minister. I realize that we are prone to thinking about grief with regard to death, but there are many other types of grief experiences that cover a lifetime. "Chocolate Cake" is a way of pointing to grief that has beginnings even in childhood, but the volume concludes with "End of the Road," the ultimate grief experience—one's own death.

Chocolate Cake and Other Losses: Poems about Grief is my invitation to you to allow yourself time to ponder your losses and to grieve that which you have lost.

Chocolate Cake

For weeks we talked about his birthday,
asked him the flavor of cake he would like
and so, for weeks, he anticipated
his special dessert with three candles on top.

We watched intently as he took the plate
eagerly in hand, joy spilling out all over his face,
but the joy was to be all too short-lived,
huge tears erupting as the cake landed on the floor.

There was no consoling him
though we tried telling him
there were plenty more slices of chocolate cake
waiting in the kitchen.

I suppose when you're three
you are wary of potentially empty, conciliatory words
and so, you simply give yourself
permission to let tears flow unchecked.

I couldn't shake the image of the three-year-old
little boy, tears spilling from his eyes.
My pressing thoughts as I lay down to sleep
were about this little boy and the future losses of his life.

A pet, struck down by a passing car?
A friend who succumbs to cancer?
A job lost through down-sizing? A home destroyed by fire?
A marriage dissolved through lack of nurture?

I cried a tear or two thinking about
the losses throughout the lifetime
of this little boy, but there is one thing—
one thing I know for sure ...

Despite his losses, he will survive so long as
he rejects empty, conciliatory words,
and so long as he
lets tears flow unchecked.

Lost Score

She had time to finish it!
Thank God for that,
but she never got to
hear it played.

How can it be?
How can it be that
we leave this life
with so much unfinished business?

And what about her?
Will she—along with her
lost score—be forgotten,
as if she never lived nor left her mark?

Wait a minute!
I just heard the news—
new residents taking on the task
of remodeling her old house.

And guess what!
Amid the dust and debris—
residue of her previous life—
they found her score.

The orchestra is playing her music—
it lives on.

She lives on!

Greenware

It was a hobby of hers—
purchasing greenware pots,
painting them, having them fired
and readied for plants they would hold.

It broke my heart
when I discovered her stash
tucked away in a corner
of the living room.

These pots and so many more
she should have had time to paint,
and so many more plants she should have
had time to encourage to grow.

Greenware—symbol of unfinished business
on this earth—and so appropriate that I
be the one to discover them,
and to grieve as I held them in my hands.

After all I, too, am her greenware,
for she never had the chance
to finish with me, to watch me grow
into the person I have become!

Christy

Young—so young,
All of life
Ahead of her.

In that brief moment
Of time she made
Her decision.

Text and drive—
How could she
Have known her
Decision made
In a moment
Would cost her parents
A lifetime
Of sadness?

Kinsley

Grief specialists have
Plenty of wisdom to offer,
"Give yourself time," they say,
"Make no big decisions abruptly."
But Kinsley couldn't imagine
Life without her,
Change nothing?
Life in the same house they shared together?
Do the same things on the same calendar
That they once created?

The house?
It was gone in a matter of a month,
His job?
He took a leave of absence,
Business as usual?
No way!

Sky diving, snow skiing,
Hiking the Appalachian Trail—
His actions and his decisions to some
Seemed foolhardy,
But somehow, through doing it all,
He decided that he could
Continue to live, even without her.

Susan

She loved daisies
More than anyone
I've ever known,
She chose daisy dishes
And listed them
On her bridal registry,
She bought daisy fabric
And sewed curtains
For her kitchen,
She cooked scrumptious meals
And served them
On her daisy dishes,
She dug in the dirt,
Planted daisies
That grew to
Amazing heights.

And to this day,
I can never
Look at a daisy
Without thinking
Of her.

Southern Lady

After his own Southern lady
passed away, he ate there
every morning—Southern Lady,
Bowdon, Georgia.

Same place, same time,
same booth, same order, so
when he died, they hung
his cap on a hook at his booth.

A Southern Goodbye

We, Southerners, are noted for our
long goodbyes—
the announcement, "We need to be going,"
while still sitting on the living room sofa,
the farewell while putting on coats,
the kisses and "see you soons"
while getting in the car,
the hearty waves and blown kisses
from passenger seats
as we drive away.

It's a hard thing to say goodbye,
and once is never enough.

So, then, how can we ever
say our goodbyes when
one of us prepares to leave
this earth and the company
with whom we have shared
life and love?

Other Shoe . . .

Should be happy today . . .

Good results on tests,
words of congratulations from doctors,
a whole year
without progression.

Tell me, then—
why do I find myself
sad, crying, unable to celebrate
even as others add their words of congratulations?

Why?
Because it's been
a whole year,
and I can only wait . . .

for the other shoe to drop!

The Old Me

I make every effort,
I try and try,
But no matter how much
I pledge to stop the clicking . . .

Site to site I navigate,
Asking plaguing questions,
Side effects of treatments, how long
Drugs can forestall the inevitable?

And most important of all,
Can you paint me a picture of the end?
And suddenly I no longer recognize
The person with the cloud hanging over her head.

And so I ask,
"Where is she?"
I want her back—
The old me!

Sunsets

We watched
as they watched
the sun setting over the ocean,
a pattern for every evening
of their lives.

Come with me,
my love,
the sunsets
are ticking by
and I only
want to be
with you
as the sun
sets over
the evenings
of our lives.

Separating

Standing on my stool
at the counter I watched,
amazed I saw Mother
separate the eggs—

Whites here, yellows there.

These years later
I work to separate
as skillfully as did
my mother—

Living here, dying there.

Assignments

Teachers make assignments,
and managers make assignments,
To whom can I assign
the work that I do—
Loving, caring for my husband,
Loving, encouraging my children,
Loving, hugging my grandchildren,
when I am no longer here?

My Tribute

What will they say
about me
after I'm gone?

That I kept
a nice house—
sometimes messy,
sometimes with laundry
piled high but still
reasonably clean?

That I played
the piano well
though sometimes
I didn't practice enough
and shied away
from pieces too hard?

That I preached quite a few sermons
though some were
less than well-prepared
and others left folks
scratching their heads.

Ah! Instead, may they say
that I touched a few lives,
that I tried to be faithful,
that I did my best
with the life
I was given.

Our History

We bought
a piece of history,
an old house
a hundred and more.

And as
we worked on
projects to be done,
we added history of our own.

Jokingly, I said that
when God calls me home
I'll have to respond, "But God
there still are jobs to be done!"

But it's no longer a joke,
I want to bargain with God.

"More, please!
More time,
more memories,
more loving,
more time to write
our history!"

A Year

Sometimes a year
seems a lifetime,
but certainly not
in this case!

It's been a year
since the doctor
hung her head
and spoke quietly.

"There's no cure,
but we can give you
some more time,
more quality time."

So how long is more?
And what do I do
with more,
and is more ever enough?

And who is out there
who has already
discovered answers
to these questions?

Please call me,
please shout my name
because I want to meet you,
I want you to hold my hand.

Figure It Out

I tell myself
that I should have
figured it out
by now ...

figured out
the things that really count,
and how to get them done,
in the allotted timeframe,
figured out how
to cope with
the feelings that well up
within me.

But then again,
why punish myself?
This task belongs in the
category of things
they should have taught
in school or if not in school.
somewhere along
life's path.

But in a class
all by itself ...

How to face death
with dignity and grace,
and with a sense of thanksgiving
for all that has been.

Ropes Course

As our ropes course guide
helped each of us
into our harnesses,
he taught us about
the importance of reliance,
not only upon harnesses and
belay persons, but also
of dependence upon one another,
communicating with one another,
calling out words of encouragement.

So when they
began their ascent
to the forty-foot-high ropes
some screamed a little,
while others simply
said how frightened
they were, and in each case
the group provided words
of encouragement,
"Come on! You can do it,
'cause we're here for you!"

But me?
Could I scream?
Could I ask for help?
as I made my way
forty feet into the air?

No! All I could do
was go silent,
So how could I expect
anyone to know
how afraid I was?

And the day
that cancer returned,
what could I do?
Scream? Ask for help?

No! All I could do
was go silent.

"Great Is Thy Faithfulness"

Who knew?
And how could he know
those many years ago—
in 1923 to be exact?
Who knew so long ago
that I—that we—would need
the words, "Strength for today
and bright hope for tomorrow?"

Truth be told,
Thomas Obadiah Chisholm
could never have imagined
all of us, the struggles we bear.

But he knew his own struggles,
and he knew his need
for strength and for hope
in the midst of it all.

And he found God to be faithful.

Bird Call

The little bird
sat on his perch,
looked my direction,
sang his song.

Engrossed in reading,
I tried ignoring,
but with a sense of urgency
his tones pierced my ears.

"Time to start,"
eagerly he said,
"living for today,
just for today."

"Worries be gone,
saved for tomorrow
or another day,
but this day . . .

This good day,
live, find happiness,
wherever and whenever,
you possibly can!"

Ticking

Do you remember
the old mantle clocks
and how they ticked loudly
whenever the family gathered
for conversation 'round the fireplace?
Sometimes the ticking
got stuck in your ears
and in your head
and you could hear nothing
other than the
tick, tick, tick—
not the words
they were saying.
All the conversation was lost
in the tick, tick, tick.

And we—those of us
who hear our diagnoses—
sometimes we get lost
in the tick, tick, tick.

But we must stop,
drown out the ticking,
listen for the sounds of today,
the conversation going on around us!

Now

Imagining that they might
Minimize the ultimate
Loss, they pulled away
From one another ...

   He from she,
   She from he.

How very sad that
Their attempts to minimize
Costs them precious moments ...

   Now.

Nevertheless

It was Good Friday and I sat
with the old man
in the waiting room as his wife
lay dying in the ICU.

"Jesus prayed," he said,
"prayed the 'let this cup
pass from me,'" And I listened,
torn with emotion.

"Over and over," he said,
"I've prayed that part
of the prayer." And I listened
this time for what would come next.

"So far," he said,
"I haven't been able
to pray the 'Nevertheless,'"
to which I responded with deafening silence.

It's all he could do—
all any of us can do.
We must sit with our,
"Take this cup from me,"

Until God grants
us strength
to finally be able
to pray the "Nevertheless."

What Is

I sat with her for what seemed
the one-hundredth time she was there
with her husband, hospitalized for chronic infection
that had landed him in a wheelchair.

"How do you do it?" I quizzed,
deep desire to know about the strength
she must summon day by day
as she cared for him.

And this is what she said
to me in response to my query,
"You learn not to worry so much
about what isn't."

"Instead, you must learn to be
thankful for what is!"
So I turned the words over and over,
and stored them for safe keeping.

Thank God that the storage was safe
because now I must be thankful for
what is without worrying so much
about what isn't.

Celebrations

Thanksgivings,
Christmases,
New Year's,
Birthdays,
Anniversaries.

We can
no longer
take additional
ones for
granted but
we can
be thankful
for ones
we have
and hope
for more!

Process

It's not the dying . . .

The side effects
   of drugs that feel
      like human experimentation,
Days spent in bed,
   living but feeling like not living
      humiliation for the time spent
         unable to care for bodily functions,
            the worry caused to loved ones,
               the slip, slip, slipping into the abyss.

It's the process.

Daffodils

When I am gone,
no need for pots of expensive flowers,
but instead, plant daffodils.
Start in my yard . . .

In the front by the edge of the road,
in the side beds recently created,
on the terraces,
in the back forty I never got cleared.

But also in the yards of neighbors,
for shut-ins still living at home,
in the courtyards of nursing homes,
in pots for nursing stations.

Wherever folks need a bit of cheer
and to be reminded of strength
and bravery for living
this life of ours, hard as it may be.

After all we invest in each other,
love each other,
and one day we are separated
by death.

But the daffodil reminds
those left behind to keep
poking heads up and spreading
beauty despite the cold, biting wind.

Little Bird

What joy for us
seeing the little bird
in its nest by the front door,
listening to him
chirp his demand for food
and watching him grow
and fluff his wings.

What sorrow for us
when one day we
came home only
to discover him gone,
no doubt spreading his wings
and flying off
to experience life in the world.

What sorrow for us
when those we love
fly off from us,
called by God
to experience life in the world beyond.

All Places on Earth

I remember a time
when I was young,
It was my first trip
to the beach
and the wind whipped
and the sand stung
and the waves raged
higher than my head,
And I recalled
Grandmother waiting
at home for me.

How homesick I was—
ready to leave
this foreign place
and rest in the arms
that loved me beyond measure.

Years later
I am happy
in that place—cherish it—
above most other places
on earth.

I find that
I want to stay
though Grandmother
eagerly waits

for me
and tells me
how much I
should look forward
to joining her
in heaven.

Lost Generation

Two family lines converge
At the fence post,
The strong hands
Of each dedicated
To fixing what
Needs fixing,
Doing what
Needs doing.

What a privilege
To picture those strong
Hands held in my own,
But I shudder to realize
That now those
Hands long past
Entrust the fixing
And the doing
To my own sometimes
Faltering hands.

Numbers

As young children we learn
To write them and recite them in order,
The older we get the more
We use them to add and to subtract.

Then later we form them into equations
And solve for the letter X,
And sometimes we toss them around mindlessly,
Giving scarcely a thought.

"How long?" I say, and she nonchalantly responds,
"Somewhere between four and ten."
Why not, then for me, a sense of calm?
After all, they're just numbers.

Except for one thing,
The numbers represent my life!

Good Intentions

"It's just hair," she exclaimed,
"and you can always find a nice wig,"
Oblivious she was to my tears,
so I blinked them diligently away.

"So, you're having a difficult day,
But good days will come too,
You should just be grateful," and I nodded,
embarrassed for my perceived lack of strength.

"Well, I know you worry
about what's ahead, but you need
to put that straight out of your head."
And I try to summon from within me new measures of courage.

Good intentions—
They all have them,
So, why, then?
Why do I feel no better?

Sweet Tea

Easy enough to see over the fence
separating our yards,
have done it hundreds
of times before.
Most times I simply
catch a glimpse of his
sneaking off to his mancave
where he will puff away
at his cancer sticks.

Only thing is—no cancer—
but meanwhile I sit
on my porch complaining
of the unfairness of the situation,
After all, haven't I
exercised, eaten well, refrained
from the vile weed?
So what fairness can there be
in my sitting here
contemplating
doctor visits, scans, and treatments.

I don't dare, but I want to,
I want to wag my finger at God,
proclaim the unfairness of it all,
insist on an explanation.

But then, in my vivid imagination
I catch a picture of God,
resting on a cloud
in a none-too-comfy lounge chair—
you know, the green and white webbed
variety from the 60's
while dressed in a Hawaiian shirt
and sipping on a glass of sweet tea!

"And, by the way," I add,
(After all when you get wound up
and on a roll with God, you might as well
get it all said in one fell swoop!)
"By the way, haven't you even noticed
that besides eating well and exercising,
I don't even drink the sweet stuff?
No, it's unsweet all the way,
so, doesn't that count for something?
I tell you, it's unfair—unfair I say!"

Then I chuckle to myself
'cause I catch a glimpse of God who's
looking my way, pushing the glass toward me,
and saying, "Well, here, have some?
It can't KILL you!"

"Very funny," I say in return,
but then I keep pressing,
"Anything else to say for yourself?
Any other grand words about fairness?"

"No! No, I guess I don't,
But sometime when you're ready
maybe we could run through your life,
motion-picture style,
and maybe we could skip here and there
with big pauses over all
the good stuff. I've been there
through thick and thin, you know!"

Not sure I'm ready for the motion picture,
I think I want to stew a bit more
on the theme of unfairness,
but one day—one day soon—
maybe I'll drink in that sweet tea
and all the goodness as well.

Who?

Who will take the phone call
and review the family recipe?
Who will cook the turkey
and make the dressing?
Who will buy the birthday cards
and slip them into the mail
to arrive just in time?
Who will listen to their
frustrations about jobs
or about children not behaving
the way they would like?
Who will tell them,
"It's all going to be okay!"
Who will hold their hands,
and tell them about my love
that will never die?

The List

"Nothing gentle about
this conversation," I say,
my voice already elevated.
"Someone might have
once called me
the gentle Gentile,
but not this time!"

I pause,
thinking an answer
is in order,
But he continues reading—
some ancient book
I surmise.

He doesn't look up,
but I think I hear
an "Uh-huh,"
coming from his direction.

That encourages me
enough that I dare continue,
"I have my list you know!"
Another pause—
a long pause—waiting
for a response.

Again I think
I hear an "Uh-huh,"
so I press on.

"I've been keeping it
a long time you know,
most everything
framed as questions
and most of them
beginning with the word,
'Why?'"

Caught up, I am,
in my own train of thought,
scarcely any ability
to listen for an answer
so this time I continue
after imagining only a nod.

This is an example,
and as if
holding the list
in my hand I say,
"Why did he have to die,"
Looking up,
again a real—maybe imagined
nod, to which I add,
"before I even
got to know him?"

My emotion intensifies, and
my voice in response
lifts to a level
definitely inappropriate

to civil conversation,
but never-you-mind,
I go on.

"Then, there's Grandmother,
gone so early,
and why did I
have to lose her,
my second mom?"

"And then there's Mom,
she, too, gone early, and
from this dreaded
disease?
And finally there's me!"

"Now I'm not saying
I'm terribly young,
and I'm not pretending
to be worse off
than many others—
you know, young,
children still to raise,
that kind of stuff!"

But why?
Why this dreaded disease,
the one that took
my mom so young,
that now will take me?"

"It's on my list!
I'm bringing it with me!
You haven't heard

the last from me!
When I get there,
I'll stand before you,
I'll stand and I'll stand
'til I get an answer!"

By this point
I'm a little weary,
(Emotion carries
that kind of weight,
you know!)
So this time I try
to be patient as
my hands clutch
the imaginary list.

Finally, exhausted—
maybe a bit
of resignation deep
within me—
I fold my hands
gently into my lap
and I nod off.

But I awake
with a start,
these words demanding
my immediate attention,
"We'll see!"
"We'll see!"

Raindrops

It's a perfect morning!

Air a bit chilly,
clouds settling in
as a blanket on this
October morning,
raindrops falling
gentle as feathers
from the sky
as if taking
their time and
finding the perfect
soft spot on which
to land.

It's a perfect morning.
My time of day,
so let me go, God,
Let me go
gently, and help
me find
my soft spot on which
to land.

But more importantly
help them,
Help them to find
their own soft spots

on which to land,
And help them—
my loves—
to awaken
to many more

Perfect mornings.

Persimmon Branch

He gave her the persimmon branch,
An investment of his time and talent.

We chuckled a bit to ourselves,
The persimmon branch,
Symbol for best wishes,
Good fortune.

We remembered how
Many times she
Collected the junk mail,
Joyous that she would
Be the winner of first one
Sweepstakes and then another.

But the persimmon branch
Pointed her in two directions—
To her past, to loved ones long gone,
Those who shared the persimmon fruit
From the old home-place on the dirt road.

But it pointed ahead,
To this new generation,
To this grandson with
The talent for painting,
To his siblings,

And even to the great-grandchildren
That she would never know.

Treasure?
Indeed!

Invest

No!
Not in 401K's,
Not in gold,
Not in silver,
No padding
the bank account.

Plant trees,
ones that won't mature
for twenty, thirty—
forty years,
Create food banks
and clothing closets
for thousands of people
in need,
Leave seed money
for scholarships
for students otherwise
unable to study,
Write a book
about all the things
you've learned
in this life
and inscribe it
with your love.

Whatever you do . . .

Invest!

Visions

Inside a segment
of my brain
lies a swirling,
hurling mass of
spirits, chaotic in
their nature,
giving me pause,
They are known,
yet still unknowing.

And I ask
the fateful question,
"Is this it—
all there is—
objects of our
lifelong hopes and
earthly religious pursuits?"

But in another
corner of my
worrying, inquiring brain
rises a hoard
of gentle, smiling
faces—masses such
as I have
never even imagined,

They are known,
but also, they
are knowing as
might be demonstrated
by their joyful
recognition as I
pass through the
gates and they,
in one accord,
say, "Welcome! We've
been expecting you!"

My Last

Not a single
thought, simply
in, out,
in, out.

But what about
the last
given me—
ponderous?
struggling?
anxiety-ridden?

Or . . .

Driven by
long anticipation,
simple repose,
medication relaxing
me into
my last?

Scriptures and a Few Prayers

"Just read scriptures and
say a few prayers," he said,
as I sat with him
planning her funeral,
"After all, she was a
mean woman, and I
don't want you
to have to lie!"

No more! No less!
Scriptures and a few prayers,
with no remembrances
of her life, so afterward
I went home to cook supper
and to ready myself for bed,
whereupon I found myself
sad, unable to shake
the weight of chilling feelings.

"What is wrong?" I asked
myself, certain the feelings
were displaced, for,
after all, she wasn't
a relative nor a friend,
but someone
I hadn't even known.

Then it occurred to me
that I carried the sadness
of a wasted life, no positive
connections even to those
entrusted to her.

The pledge made to myself
as I lay down to sleep
was to make my days count,
especially in investments
in people around me.

The Porch

We sat on our porch
through a gentle spring
and a long a luxurious summer,
basking in the sights and sounds
of the neighborhood.

Confident we were
of weathering the seasons,
sitting side by side
on the porch,
but one day it became clear
that we must prepare for winter,
fortify ourselves
against the cold.

And so we broke
the heater out,
dust mites and all,
from its storage,
a relic in the attic,
It was a joke against ourselves
that such fortification
is possible,
that one can
cheat the winds
that beat against
tired bodies
while sitting on the porch.

Look Up

Look up!
Tiny buds are forming,
and we will
watch them intently
every single day,
gazing as
they unfold
into glorious green.

Look up!
Green is
in its fullness
and delights
us with
its grandeur.

Look up!
Orange, red, gold—
truly you have
become what you
were designed
to be,
and we sit
in amazement
through a grand
and glorious season.

But then—
no one calls,
"Look up!"
Even I rush
along, keeping
my eyes focused
straight ahead,
For there is
something intimidating
to all of us
about this season of life.

But maybe—
just maybe we
can learn to
cherish it,
After all, this season is
never over and
done, but rather it
leads to a
glorious future.

I Wonder

I wonder what each
is feeling
with the
drip, drip, drip
going into an arm.

Worry?
Desperate clinging
to bits of hope?
Resignation that what is
is what is?

In other rooms
they undress,
put on the garb
that now
has become familiar,
this process taking
far longer
than the laser-beamed
precision of the radiation
toward its
designated spot.

Occasionally those
sitting in the room
with the drip, drip, drip
hear the familiar

ring of the bell
hung nearby
on the wall.

Most stop
their reading or knitting,
or they peel their eyes
away from the screen
long enough to clap
their congratulatory gestures,
Inside, though, some
are wondering,
"But for how long
will there be cause
for celebration?"

Sometimes I wish
that I could
talk with each
one of them,
hear their stories,
but then I am
sure that I
have not the
strength to absorb
their collective sadness.

Carpenter Shop

The characteristic whines
Of drills and saws
Fill the ears of all
Who work nearby.

They recognize them
As tools of the trade,
The carpenter, the shops
They remember from childhood.

But they have moved on—
He has moved on and
This is no ordinary
Brand of carpentry.

No sawing nor drilling
On pieces of wood,
No crafting useful things
Like tables and chairs.

Instead, most days this tradesman
Cuts out the old
And painstakingly transplants
The new—hips and knees mostly.

There's joy in the work,
Restoring levels of function,
But this day there are waves of sadness
As he takes tools in hand.

So, he whispers a silent prayer
For this young one who will
Wake up minus an arm, that God will redeem
The loss by granting her more years on this earth.

What We Make of Them

She awoke from the anesthesia,
Sipped on her ice chips,
Took the pain meds
As directed by the RN.

She might have been angry,
Stuck in the midst of
Bitterness and resentment,
Unable to move ahead.

After all, they misdiagnosed her,
Delayed treatment, sent her home
Saying she had pulled a muscle,
Likely from her work.

Then it was too late,
Save for radical surgery,
Yet, when interviewed decades later
She proudly displayed her prosthesis.

She continued in the same job,
Said she hated the word, "handicapped,"
It's not always our losses
But what we make of them.

Dementia

She left
little bit
by little bit,
day by day
until nothing of her
remained.

She lived five years
longer.

Freshman Year

No time for feelings
To rise to the surface—
Last-minute shopping,
Establishing checking accounts,
Paying tuition, room, and board,
Packing and re-packing
Everything into the car.

But then there's their arrival,
Unpacking the car, and
All too soon she's ready
To say goodbye and send Mom on her way.

Then? Then there's time—
All the way home in fact—
To let feelings rise to the surface.

Stewart

He filed them away,
memories of the war,
though his injuries
were their own
everyday kinds
of reminders.

Something about
his last days
unlocked some
of the memories,
but still the
words he shared
were few
and far between.

"Battle of the Bulge,"
he said, "I was there,
spent time in foxholes,
shoes and socks wet,
chilled to the very bone!"

"Never," he said,
"Never again do I want
my feet to be wet."

Donald and Ellis

Donald—a paraplegic from an accident at work,
Donald—a guy not given to new-fangled equipment,
    demanding not a power-chair,
    when a manual will do.
Ellis—He looks the same as always on the outside,
    and on good days, he can convince you
    nothing is wrong,
    Other days there's no doubt that
    plenty is wrong,
    His doctor pronounced it Alzheimer's.

Sunday mornings Ellis, in his Silverado,
would drive the few miles to Donald's house,
where Donald, in his chair, would latch on,
driver's side window,
After all, the hill that crested
at the driveway of the church proved
too much, even for Donald's strong arms.

On mornings when I was privy to the scene
playing out before my eyes,
my mind took a flight of fantasy,
and I was sure that Donald and Ellis
were not simply cresting the top of the hill
and entering the church yard, but rather
they were entering the very gates of heaven,
both of them made whole,
Donald's legs and Ellis' brain.

Joshua

We like to pretend
It's just the naughty kids
Who get into trouble,
The bully who finally
Meets his match,
The girl who
Sneaks out of her
Bedroom window
In the middle
Of the night,
But then there's . . .

Joshua,
Named for the one
Who would walk the final
Miles into the
Promised Land.

It was a youth group event,
He straddled his cycle,
Fearlessly made his jump,
And the rest is history.

No possibility to walk
Those miles to the Promised Land,
Made a paraplegic at age eighteen.

Pop

He joined the Merchant Marines,
Came home, settled in, became a supervisor
In the cotton mill, gave thirty-plus years
To the work he loved,
Then what?
How to fill the hours?
They gave him the keys
To the floral delivery truck,
Work he also came to love,
Three fender-benders later,
They took his keys away,
Then what?
How to fill the hours?
He walked every day to the ballfield
A few blocks from home,
Met friends there, old guys just like himself,
They dubbed the place the United Nations,
And there they solved the problems
Of the world.

To Work

They said horrible
things to him,
like, "Wish I had
your problem!
What I wouldn't
give to be
able to retire!
Why, I'd sleep
'til noon,
go on cruises,
eat, sleep, and
be merry!"

What they didn't
know was that
he didn't know
who he was
apart from a person
who got up
early and went
to work every
single day!

Hope

Newspaper reporters
Were there
And they watched
As she sifted
Through the debris.

Most everything—
All her inventory,
The things that
Had claimed her
Financial resources
As well as her
Endless hours of
Work—were
Unrecognizable,
Dusty grains
Of charcoal, but
Just as she was
Ready to go home,
Fix a cup
Of tea, sit
On the couch,
Cry her eyes out,
She stopped, bent down,
Picked up a figure,
Charred but still
Intact, and she
Ran her fingers

Over the Willowtree
Angel, especially the
Arms lifted to
Heaven—the figure
Hope.

She went home,
Fixed a cup
Of tea, cried
Some tears, but
As she clutched
Hope she was
Certain that she
Could rebuild.

Curiosity Seekers

We couldn't help ourselves,
Emergency management folks
Had asked everyone
To stay home—
To stay out of their way.

But, of course, as soon as
The roads were clear
Droves of people
Showed up to see
What they could see.

Mostly they gathered
Near the river whose
Force still carried
Pieces of people's lives.

We knew it was time
To go home when
We saw a refrigerator
Floating past, a reminder
That a refrigerator
Is not just
A refrigerator but part of
Someone's dream,
Carried away as if
Nothing at all.

The Way Home

As she lay dying
She occasionally sat
Bolt-upright in bed
And said, "Look at them!
Angels! Aren't they beautiful?"
But the exclamations
Embarrassed her family,
And they were known
To shake their heads
And apologize to visitors
That she was talking
Out of her head.

What's wrong with us?
Why apologize?
Why not make room for
Angels come to be
With the dying and to
Show them the way home?

An Archaeologist

Today I became an archaeologist,
Digging ivy from my backyard
I found iron hooks and glass bottles,
even a piece of large pottery.

Could I find all the broken parts and piece them together,
Could the not-really-an-archaeologist take it to the experts
    for dating,
or should I make a trip to Antiques Road Shop and, hope-
    against-hope,
listen for a value that would make my jaw drop?

I like my pretend-to-be an archaeologist self,
I like old hooks and bottles and pottery,
but after my flights of fantasy, I decided to give more
    thought,
not to the things, but to the people who shared time in my
    old house.
What were their hopes, their dreams?

As I dig in the dirt, I realize how connected
we all are, and how, in the end, we, too,
find our places in the dirt.

Messages

"Gotta stay busy," they say,
As if busyness could ever wipe away
The thoughts whirling in my brain.

"She wouldn't want you to be sad," they say,
As if I need guilt about the potential to
Disappoint her—especially now.

"Ya just have to move on," they resolve,
As if grief is simply a package you wrap up
And store away in the attic.

My Sadness

My sadness makes them all nervous,
And so they try to help me forget it,
Act as though it's business as usual.

"They're developing new treatments every day!"
"No one knows the timetable—only God!"
"I could die before you do!"
"We could all head out from here
And get hit by a bus!"

But what I know is this—
If I don't get hit by a bus
This dreaded disease will be
The end of me!

The Brave

"A coward," he says,
"dies a thousand deaths,"
Then he continues,
"but the brave die but one!"

So he thinks
persons wake up
in the morning
facing a tragedy
and they choose—
choose to be either
cowards or bravehearts?

Maybe—just maybe—
he is wrong,
and maybe—just maybe–
it's a process,
maybe some must die
those thousand deaths,
and in so doing,
become brave.

Sleeth

Sleeth says it best,
"In the end is the beginning,
In the seed an apple tree,"
She offers it for us to sing.

She is right, you know,
There are always endings,
and you and I—we get caught up—
caught up in the sadness of them all . . .

So caught up that we rarely
notice the new beginnings,
but they are happening all around us,
if only we are attentive, eyes open to see.

I visited the grandmother
dying in her hospital bed,
family gathered all around, when,
above their quiet sobs, I heard a wail.

It was a demand for air,
a demand for everyone to stand up
and take notice of the miracle occurring
in the delivery room down the hall.

Sleeth said it best as she offered
her words in song, but I'll say it again,
Rather I'll sing them
from the bottom of my heart,

"In the end is the beginning,
In the seed an apple tree!"

Terminal

Our trip took us
through small towns
and smaller towns, one, once upon a time,
a thriving railroad stop.

And once upon a time
an entrepreneur, drawing upon
his best creative juices, dubbed his cafe,
the Terminal Cafe.

We've laughed and told the story
time and time again,
So, what was he thinking?—links, for us,
not to the railroad terminal but to food that kills!

Terminal—a seemingly innocent word,
a word that inspires storytelling
and lots of laughter,
but today, in a different context,

The word brings no laughter.

How?

How can we grieve it all?
How can we grieve the sadness
of homes lost to earthquakes, floods, and fires,
and worse still all the lives that are lost?

And worse still, how can we
grieve the sadness of violence done
person to person, family member to family member,
and student to student?

We know the dangers of
turning a blind eye,
know that so easily we can become unfeeling,
calloused to the losses of people around us,
but the losses—they happen so often.

We can scarcely take them in,
much less let our hearts
feel the depth of emotion
of people around us.

How?
How can we grieve it all?

How Much?

The Psalmist did not mind,
In a demanding tone, to ask of God,
"How long? How long, O God?"
Thinking it inappropriate, you and I are far more cautious.

Her phone call came late at night,
Just what we'd been expecting,
Word that his cancer
had finally won out.

The second, a few months later,
Came, a jolting reality,
So much so that I
Could scarcely take it in.

"Ryan's dead," she said, "plowed into by a senior adult
as they headed to the prom."
To this day I can never be certain
what words came out of my mouth . . .

But one thing I know for sure,
I wanted to speak with God,
Anger barely disguised, and to demand,
"How much can any one individual endure?"

This Day

I need this day,
this day of peace,
quiet,
sunshine.

I need this day
to cast aside
sadness for what has been,
worry for what is ahead.

So I am committed,
I will push them away—
sadness, worry—with all the strength
within me I will banish them.

And I will sit in the quiet,
this day of peace and tranquility,
and I will let the sunshine bathe me
and bring refreshment to my weary soul.

I will treasure—
treasure this day
with no thought for the future,
for this day—it is a gift.

The You I Never Knew

As I grew a sadness came over me,
but they said it couldn't
be because of the loss of you, for, after all,
I was so little when you were gone.

Trouble is that every day I heard
about their loss, about their sadness,
and I heard about how much you loved me,
and even about how much I looked like you.

When I see pictures of you, me in your arms,
I can feel that little girl and also your love,
So I will continue to believe that your staying with me
would have changed my life for good.

The sadness—
the sadness about the you I never knew?
For now I'll let it
stay with me.

They Say

They say . . .
They always have something to say,
no matter what the topic.

They say you should never
begrudge a guy the chance
to get away a bit,
escape his responsibilities.

They say you should have no regrets
when the guy—no matter how young—
dies doing what it is he loves best.

They say it was a freak accident,
the way the lantern overturned,
They say you should have
made it out, you and your buddies.

They say you were a good swimmer,
that you must've gotten cramps,
They say, "Cryin' shame you left the boat,
'cause it didn't even burn all the way!"

I Say

I say . . .

Wish you'd stayed home,
maybe just a short trip
to Smith Drug to buy two Whitman samplers
and cards with mushy rhymes.

I say we'll spend a lifetime
trying to forgive you,
one spending the rest of her days saying,
"A mother shouldn't have to bury her son,"
Another saying, "How do I raise
two children alone?"
Another saying, "Wish he could have taken me
fishing!"
Another nodding sadly, "If only . . .
if only I could have known him!"
And all of them silently saying,
"Wish we didn't every year, the second Sunday of
May,
have to be reminded,
Mother's Day—the day they recovered
your body!"

PTSD

He was one of the lucky ones
They said, first,
That he came home at all,
Then with his fingers and toes,
Arms and legs intact.

But when a thunderstorm arose
Or a neighbor shot off fireworks,
Someone had to talk him down,
Evenings were the worst,
Sleep punctuated by his own screams,
But even more than that was the night
When muffled sounds awakened him,
His hands around her neck.

Lucky?
If only they knew.

Fidelity

We watched as the boxes
Extended further and further
Along the lawn,
And we couldn't help
But feel sorry for him,
If only a bit,

Evicted
By his own life partner.

We couldn't help
But feel sorry for her
Too, for we knew the depths
Of her sadness,
Her feelings of betrayal,
How many times she asked,

"Whatever happened to fidelity?"

It's Over

Quickly she typed
The words, "It's over,"
And instantly we received
Them and stepped into action.

We left the party,
It was supposed to be
A happy time,
A holiday season.

But since when
Do things turn out
The way they're supposed to?
Certainly not for them.

That night we started
A process—walking and talking,
Walking and talking—how many miles
We logged, I can't be sure.

But would there ever
Have been healing,
Ability to turn the page,
Start a new chapter without . . .

Walking and talking.

Sad about Dad

"Hurry," Mom yelled,
"You've got to get to school, and
I can't be late for work, so
grab your things and let's go!"

At school the teacher yelled,
"Haven't I told you
a million times not
to show up unprepared?"

The lunchroom lady yelled,
"Can't you ever remember
to get your mom to write a check?
Money doesn't grow on trees you know!"

The bus driver yelled
across the parking lot, "Hurry, hurry, hurry!
We can't keep waiting,
Gotta get everyone home!"

What they didn't know was
that Mom and Dad argued last night,
and that Dad left—not sure
if he's ever coming back.

Don't Tell Me

His grandmother
Took care of him,
Held him in her lap,
Fed him his bottle,
And his first
Spoons-ful of cereal,
Sang to him,
Rocked him to sleep
In her antique rocker.

His mother tells the story
That he cried non-stop
For six months
As soon as her mother
Passed away.

Don't tell me
That babies
Never grieve!

War-Torn Wedding

Choosing the right venue
Takes an eternity
For the bride-to-be,
Visiting churches, historic buildings,
Victorian homes—any place
Of great beauty, for,
After all, this place
Represents the beginning
Of their lives
Together.

We watched the news,
Saw the venue
For this young couple
Saying their vows
In front of the rubble
That is their country
Now.

They said their "I do's,"
Held one another in a long embrace,
Kissed each other,
And then he headed
Off to serve his country,
Both of them unsure
If they would ever
See one another
Again.

Dissidents

Political dissidents,
They were forced
To flee, he a chemist
And she a doctor.

Thankful for safe
Passage to the States,
For a rented apartment
And secondhand furniture
From the sponsoring church,
They settled into their jobs,
He a maintenance worker
At the university
And she a nursing tech
At the hospital.

Standing In

We knew that it
Shouldn't be us
But rather they,
Her parents, who
Held this beautiful
Baby as she
Breathed her struggling
Breaths in her few
Short hours on this earth.

They simply couldn't
Take in the reality,
The long years of
Trying to get pregnant,
But a pregnancy
That was picture-perfect
Right 'til delivery
When a virus passed
From mom to baby,
Too much for her tiny heart.

"Hold her," the nurses encouraged,
"Can we bring her to you,
Let you hold her
As we baptize her?" I asked.

The pain was too much and so
They shut themselves
Off, thinking the distance
Would ease their heartache.

The staff watched
As I read the liturgy
And sprinkled water
On her head, and
Then we took turns
Holding her, talking to her
Until she breathed
Her last.

Standing in for others—
We need to be ready.

A Building/A Beam/A Rope

He was gone, her youngest,
Lost to a building,
A beam, and a rope.

She contemplated taking it down,
Lest it be a constant reminder
Of her loss, but oh, so impractical,
Her need for storage winning out in the end.

Though there was nothing
He could have done, the older brother
Blamed himself, but he managed to live
Under the cloud for decades longer
Until darkness finally overcame him.

He was gone, her remaining son,
Lost to a building, a beam,
And a rope.

Our Clue

We beat ourselves up,
And asked,
"Why didn't we pay
Closer attention?"

More than anything she loved
That dog,
That she had adopted only
Months earlier,

Said she had found him a
New home,
And that clearly should have been
Our clue.

Richard B. Russell Highway

Despondent,
Unable to see how things might get any
Better,
She plotted her
Escape,
Concern for appearances, it must need be an
"Accident," clear loss of
Control.

Ah! The Richard B. Russell Highway—twists and
Turns,
The best place to stage her
Demise,
"But wait a minute! They might need the
Car!"

Up the next day she focused on making it 'til things would get
Better.

Channeling

Their energies had to go somewhere,
Otherwise, they might turn them
On each other, or on themselves,
Anger chipping away from the inside out.

They showed up every day in the courtroom,
Silent prayers for a lifetime conviction,
They prepared victim statements, with pictures
Of him, their only son.

They attended every parole hearing,
Decried the injustice—a life snuffed out
Before getting much of a start,
Meanwhile, this so-called friend . . .

Still living and breathing.

Forgive

A hard thing—to forgive.
A near impossibility—to forgive one
    who hurts your child.
A clear impossibility—to forgive yourself
    complicity in hurting your own child.

They got the phone call,
Rushed to the hospital,
Listened to officers,
Took in details as best they could,
Shook their heads in disbelief,
Shot at point-blank range,
Suspect taken into custody,
His friend—his very best friend!

The gun?
A service revolver from their own closet.

Distance Grief

It doesn't have to happen
In our own homes,
To our own families, to the people
Who live next door.

The family in Georgia
Turns on their TV and watches
As a young man enters a school
In Uvalde to inflict his treachery.

Family members in Nebraska
Heat their food and then gather
For the evening news and watch racist vigilantes
Chase down a young black man, shooting him in the back.

A young guy working in New York City
Stops for a sandwich and sees the reports
Of young men in Ukraine donning weapons
Of war to defend against Russian aggression.

We grieve, not only for ourselves,
Not only for those close to home,
But for those even in far-flung
Places across the globe.

Tsunami

All our losses are
A bit like a tsunami,
The impending storm, or death, or threat of war,
Are like the wall of water, gathering its force.

But in a moment of time,
Before we can begin to prepare ourselves,
The waters sweep in and gather
Everything in their wake.

Then they recede and we are left
With a vast nothingness.

No Buttons/No Zippers

Disaster hit
And left them
With no homes,
No clothes
Except the ones
On their backs.

Missionaries prayed
With them, encouraged
Them to hold on,
Promised that relief
Organizations in the U.S.
Were sending shipments
Of supplies.

The shipment arrived
As promised—clothes–
Mountains of them ...

Minus their buttons
And zippers.

Walking and Talking

Sometimes walking and talking
Provide far more
Than simple points
Recorded on a FitBit.

Long before there were FitBits,
We walked a lot,
Sketching our dreams
For life with one another.

But this day the walking and talking
Included many tears
And words about how the relationship
Was doomed, too much interference from family.

Thank God for his strength,
In those moments of incredible grief,
How he literally turned them
And continued the walking . . .

The talking through her feelings
That resulted in re-commitment
To relationship despite family objections,
Just think—without walking and talking . . .

We wouldn't be here,
Three children,
Twelve grandchildren,
Fifty years later.

Tiptoe

I tiptoed from one
End of the house
To the other,
No surprise in that.

Little kids love to tiptoe,
Why? I don't know,
To strengthen foot muscles?
Something else altogether?

I'll go with the latter,
For these decades later—
Near the end of my decades—
I realize something . . .

I tiptoed around them
All of my days,
And I wish we all
Could just have been real.

The Day We Stop Feeling

It's a real temptation—
a real temptation
to turn off the news,
and to almost go into hiding.

For there is a pain we can see in the lives of others—
even in those whose names we may never call—
and it taps on our shoulders,
and hangs a dark cloud over our heads.

Reminds me of when I was a child and afraid,
I simply told myself that
any part of me underneath the bedcovers
could know no harm.

And so when I visited
Grandmother's and slept
in a dark bedroom I made certain
to pull the sheet up clear over my head!

We could let this be our
operational mode throughout life—
turning off the news, doing whatever is necessary
to distance from the pain of others.

There's only one problem,
When we fail to feel with our brothers and sisters,
when we distance from their hurt, injustice, and loss,
then we stop being human.

Promise of Heaven

I shrank into the background
as my newly-found, fundamentalist
friends spoke of their great
anticipation of going home to be with God.

Though some not-small guilt
swept through me, embarrassment
that perhaps my faith was not
of the same variety as was theirs,
I could not go there.

Honesty would not allow me
to proclaim my anticipation for heaven
when clearly such a feeling evaded
my 21-year-old, still-have-much-living-to-do self.

It is decades later, and part of me still wants
to shrink into the background when the topic comes up—
the great desire to go home to be with God,
but some things have changed.

I no longer have to doubt my faith,
It's been present, good times, bad times,
past and present, but God has given me
all of you, and it's hard to leave
the warm arms of those you love,

Even with the promise of heaven,
and the hope of resting in the arms of God.

The Steeple

Sadness abounds
As we look around us,
Battleship-grey walls
That long ago needed
A fresh coat of paint,
Heat and air systems
That grunt and groan
And resist cranking
Up upon demand,
Kitchen facilities that
Exude some sort
Of dire warning,
A roof that sends
Trickles down interior walls
Each time it rains.

Easily we could find ourselves
Depressed, disparaging an old
Facility quite beyond
The financial means
Of its members.
Yet, all we need do
Is to look up!

We need see the hundred-plus-year-old
Steeple as it reaches—
Reaches boldly
Toward the sky!

Sadness abounds for us,
Years gone by,
Accumulated losses,
Bitter disappointments,
Aching bodies,
Dire diagnoses,
Grave concerns about
What lies ahead.

But despite sadness,
Disappointments,
Concerns—
All is not lost
So long as
Our heads and hearts
Reach as boldly heavenward
As does the aging steeple!

Day After

It's the day after,
day after a tragedy,
So what do you do?
steps one, two, three, tell me please.

Take a deep breath,
Take stock, survey your loss,
Then give yourself permission,
permission to cry your eyes out.

Then what?
What next?
What follows
steps one, two, three?

Make a list . . .
things to be done?
Gather your resources, coping mechanisms
as well as people to help you through?

Yes, all well and good,
but never—never forget—
that as long as necessary
repeat steps one, two, and three.

A Plan

Hundreds . . . maybe thousands
of times she told us
her plans and
instructed us in how
to carry them out.

"Have a nice service,"
she said and read
1 Thessalonians 4,
For, you see,
I will be asleep,
asleep in the Lord.

She went on,
"Bury me in Woodruff,
next to Jim,
We planned that
long ago, and
there's a spot
for you too.

Still there was more,
"Go to my cedar chest,
and find there a
Shadowline box tucked
neatly near the bottom."

"The contents? Blue, my favorite color,
And I want to be buried
In it. Remember—not dead
but merely asleep,
in the Lord."

At the time her words
seemed morbid,
not to mention too far in the future
for us to concern ourselves,
for, after all, she would be with us
a thousand years to come,
So we brushed her words aside,
a few carefully-placed "Uh-huhs"
in the course of her speech.

But the thousand years—
and even MORE—
have long since come
and gone, and I ask
myself, "Do you have
a plan?" and then
I simply marvel as
I think of her,
"Ah! Faith!"

I Remember

Take my ashes
back to Woodruff,
Etch the stone,
my beginning and my ending,
Go to the Beacon,
Order the slice-o'-plenty
along with some onion rings,
and glasses of sweet tea,
Offer some toasts and
tell your stories
that begin with,
"I remember . . ."

End of the Road

We travel
mountain roads,
never knowing where
we are going,
Sometimes,
with no warning—
no signs,
nothing to indicate
the end of the road
ahead—
there we are,
The pavement ends
and we sit
in puzzlement,
wondering
how this
can have happened.

And so it is
in life,
So it is
when we least
expect it,
we find ourselves
there—
at the end
of the road.

Notes

In "The Brave," the words "A coward dies a thousand deaths, but the brave die but once" are those of Shakespeare in *Julius Caesar*.

"Nevertheless" is a reminder of Jesus' prayer in the Garden of Gethsemane recorded in Matthew 26:39, Mark 14:36, and Luke 22:42. (KJV)

"Sleeth" is a reference to American composer Natalie Sleeth. The poem references words from "Hymn of Promise," written in 1986.

Thomas Obadiah Chisholm, American hymn writer, wrote the words to "Great Is Thy Faithfulness" in 1923. The poem, entitled after the hymn, references Chisholm's words from verse 3, "Strength for today and bright hope for tomorrow."

About the Author

Shirley Biggerstaff Wright grew up in Western North Carolina, but she has spent the majority of her life in Georgia. She studied theology at Emory University and became a United Methodist minister. Her love of pastoral care took her into many encounters with individuals who were grieving. Her DMin dissertation, completed at Erskine Theological Seminary, involved a grief support group studying and reflecting on lament Psalms. Her love of encounters with people is what has prompted much of her writing.

Wright is married to her soulmate, The Reverend Dr. Ken Wright. They have three adult children and twelve grandchildren.

9 781666 736076